# JERUSALEM X-FACTOR

Printed in the United States of America

Honor Publishing Co.
P.O.Box 1825
Fletcher, NC 28732

*Special thanks to Genell for her kind attention to every detail.*

# JERUSALEM X-FACTOR

*I dedicate this book first to my two sons of whom I am proud of each and every day and especially to my precious wife of over 30 years who always encourages me to finish what I start!*

# JERUSALEM X-FACTOR

## R A. CUEVAS

HONOR PUBLISHING COMPANY

*"I have published with the voice of thanksgiving, making known all thy wondrous works."*

- Psalms 26:7

Contents

# EDITORS NOTE:

Due to the excellent book reviews of
**"Jerusalem X-Factor"** and due to the urging
of some who have a continual concern about
the events surrounding Israel, I have decided
to update and publish this second edition.

The areas covered should take us to the
Fall of 2013. It is my intention to include
exclusively those events that bring the most
devastating and record-breaking disasters this
country has ever experienced as it relates to
official United States policy regarding
Israel's land." Jerusalem itself remains in my
forty years of discovery, a national and
international source of hope and contention.

This morning, July 1, 2013 at the
conclusion of Secretary of State John Kerry's
return from Israel, The Worst Firefight
Disaster in Arizona's recent history killed
nineteen elite firefighters. There to restart
peace talks and applying undue demands on
Israel to stop housing construction on their
land, we saw a half of town destroyed by
wildfires started by a lightning strike. The
blaze is zero percent contained as I write and
the temperatures in the state reached one

hundred degree Fahrenheit with a world record expected for today!  Israel Today is reporting June 25, "Netanyahu agrees with Kerry's peace talk terms."

**'Netanyahu is also said to be ready to halt all Jewish construction   outside of major settlement blocs in Judea and Samaria, the so-called "West Bank" that the Palestinians claim for their future state. Israeli officials have already acknowledged that a de-facto construction freeze is in place.'**

While it is my purpose to show correlations to our current climate of unprecedented disasters as it relates to our flawed foreign policy, particularly in regards to Israel, I am in no way stating that every single disaster that strikes our country is a direct result of policy.   It shall also be pointed out that in no way is this book intended to malign a particular administration. Documented  disasters in this book that present an eerie connection to the timing of national policy in regards to Israel cover past and present administrations regardless of party affiliation.
R.A. Cuevas

# PREFACE

We have a court system designed to hold criminals and law-breakers accountable for their actions but who will hold governments and kingdoms responsible for their actions? Many have theories why our country is experiencing serious decline such as abortion laws or racial bias.... However, there is no issue that invites divine retribution as when our leaders prevail upon Israel to hand over vital parts of her homeland.

**C.H. Spurgeon shared a message on July 12, 1885, titled *"Judgment of the Nations."* Excerpts of his message are as follows:**

**"There is a judgment also passing upon nations, for as nations will not exist as nations in another world, <u>they have to be judged and punished in this present</u> state. The thoughtful reader of history will not fail to observe how sternly this justice had dealt with empire after empire, when they have become corrupt. Colossal dominions have withered to the ground when sentenced by the King of kings. Go and**

ask to-day, 'Where is the empire of Assyria? Where are the mighty cities of Babylon? Where are the glories of the Medes and Persians? What has become of the Macedonian power? Where are the Caesars and their palaces?'... The omnipotent Judge has not ceased from His sovereign rule over kingdoms, and our own country may yet have to feel his chastisements. What is there about London {United States} that it should be more enduring than Rome? What are we? What is there about our boastful race, on this side of the Atlantic, or the other, that we should monopolize the favor of God? **If we rebel, and sin against Him, he will not hold us guiltless, but will deal out impartial justice to an ungrateful race." [1]**

Let's have a look at the aforementioned violation against God's laws. Surely the serious reader will take notice of sudden catastrophes that have befallen America due to the absence of Biblical considerations when dealing with Israel and especially Jerusalem!

*"I will bless them that bless you, and curse them that curse you"* (Genesis 12:3).

This was God's promise to His friend Abraham. This man was chosen by God to be the father of all who would believe upon the Living God! More importantly, he would be the man through whom the *"Anointed One,"* would one day be born into the world to bring redeeming grace to all men. The only requirement was to believe in the same manner that Abraham believed.

It should be noted that throughout the history of Abraham there has not been a nation or tribe that has experienced such violent hatred and yet been so resilient as to maintain its original culture, language, and faith as has Israel.

God's call upon Abraham would come with a promise that is still in force today! He assured him that He would hold to account any man or nation who either blessed Abraham or cursed him.

Ingrained in our national conscious is the heartfelt belief and hope that God still bestows His blessing upon our country. Attend any major sporting event and you are likely to hear the song, *"God Bless America."*

It seems that in the recent past we have made it our national policy to bless Israel and as a result we have incurred the protection of a grateful God.

One only needs to consider modern history to see how the conferred blessing or cursing works. When Jews were facing extinction at the hands of Germany's Hitler in the 1940's, many were blaming the Jews for amongst other things, crucifying the Son of God. Many did not even consider their own personal transgressions when holding to account a guilty party!

The *Holocaust*, a Hebrew term which means, "A burnt offering or sacrifice to God," resulted in untold suffering and death for the descendants of Abraham. In a notable turn of events, after World War II, it was Germany that faced isolation and demise while Israel was furnished with a title deed by the United Nations in May of 1948. This became the official recognition of *Israel* as the internationally recognized homeland for the Jews.[2]

The United States was a huge advocate in this prophetic and amazing event. Never in the history of mankind has a nation or empire lost its homeland for over 2000 years only to have it restored again! Immediately and on the very next day after receiving their land, Israel was attacked by their Arab neighbors.

The land since the days of the Romans has been mostly barren and unfruitful. Since the spring of 1948, the desert land began to bloom like a rose in a well-watered garden.

Many of the Arabs who lived on the land during the interim period were known to practice *"cross-cutting"* which is the removal of forestry for immediate economic gain. This only increased the dry and arid conditions and made the land unprofitable for growing and harvesting fruits and vegetables.

Since the time that Israel was installed back into her homeland and since 1948, rainfall has steadily increased at an annual rate of 10 percent. In other words, measured rainfall increases an average of 10 percent each and every year that Israel is in control of the land! [3]

I remember while visiting Israel in 2000 having a look into the water just before entering a boat to sail upon the Sea of Galilee. From my vantage point, I witnessed the waters teeming with fish! It was as many as I have ever seen in one place. All I could think of was the report that the 12 spies brought back to Moses after being sent to the Promised Land 3500 years ago. They described a land of *milk* and honey with luscious fruit and great abundance!

On another day while traveling by bus along the countryside I noticed a long line of box trucks laden with fruit sitting on the side of the road. I asked our tour guide, Motti, who was true Israeli and a war veteran of the 1967 war, where this large caravan of trucks was heading? "Oh," he said, "These trucks will take produce to all of the neighboring Arab-states. The neighbors here love us because we know how to work the land and we share much of it with them! Unfortunately, most people only hear from the radical minority who hate us, but the reality is that our neighbors truly love us and we get along well with them!"

*"The desert shall blossom like a rose"
(Isaiah 35:1).*

As was mentioned earlier and is worth repeating, there is one thing in common with the record- breaking disasters our nation has recently endured. Our leaders were busy pressuring and in many cases threatening Israel to trade her land for peace. How much land do we have to lose before we finally get it? Why do our leaders pretend to have the savvy and wisdom to bring an end to a conflict that dates back to Abraham's two sons, one by a freewoman, Sarah (Isaac) and one by a bond-woman, Hagar (Ishmael). Most biblical scholars agree that the beginning of Middle East conflict began at this juncture in Israel's history. Ishmael represents today's Arab people and Isaac represents all Jewish people.

Becoming respectful of history and ancient covenants will enable our nation to get back on a firm footing of the prosperity and freedoms we have enjoyed and helped export to the rest of the world! The very best we can do as voters is to elect men/women who truly love Israel and will, at best be a friend to her or at the least allow her to make decisions based on her own self-interests.

Shortly after commencing the writing of this book, I surprisingly came across excerpts from the book, *Eye to Eye, Facing the Consequences of Dividing Israel*, by White House Correspondent William Koenig. In his book, he proves many disasters befalling America come in immediate response to George H. Bush, Bill Clinton, and George W. Bush's devotion to robbing Israel of their God-given land. I am advocating in their defense that they must have been ignorant to a greater purpose at stake.

Koenig documents the following incredible facts occurred because of America's pressure on Israel to evacuate from much of their most valued land.

* Nine of the 10 costliest insurance events in U.S. history.

* Six of the 7 costliest hurricanes in U.S. history.

* Three of the 4 largest tornado outbreaks in U.S. history. Note: This does not take into account the most recent unprecedented 600 plus tornadoes that struck American soil in the month of April, 2011. (So, 4 of the last 5 to date).

*The two largest terrorist attacks in U.S. history.

Amazon.com says, **"All of these major catastrophes occurred on the very same day or within 24 hours of presidents Bush, Clinton, and Bush applying pressure on Israel to trade her land for promises of peace and security.** [4]

The events in his book were published in 2004 predating documentation that I began in August of 2005. I chose to include some of his observations in the *introduction* along with personal commentary rather than reinvent the wheel and omit such relevant corresponding events.

R.A.Cuevas

"THE RIGHTEOUSNESS OF THY
TESTIMONIES ARE EVERLASTING.
GIVE ME UNDERSTANDING THAT
I MAY LIVE."

-PSALMS 119:144

# INTRODUCTION

## "THEY HAVE DIVIDED UP MY LAND."
### (Joel 3:2)

In this passage, we receive a glimpse into God's intentions for Abraham and his descendants. This land was never to be broken up into pieces! He partitioned this small coastal tract of land and drew up the property lines Himself. It should also be noted that God calls this "*My land*," thus signifying His right to give it to whosoever He wills.

Every time our elected officials demand or pressure Israel to give up *pieces* of land, we here in America suffer the loss of pieces of our own real estate. Beginning with George H. Bush and his signing of the infamous *Oslo Accord* on October 30, 1991, major catastrophes have occurred simultaneously in America. According to the agreement, Israel was to swap land for peace.

19

The premise was simply, *"Give us your land and we will stop killing you."* At the time, the Oslo Accord seemed like the perfect political solution but on the very next day, October 31, a storm of epic proportions hit the United States. [1]

## OSLO ACCORD october 30, 1991
## THE PERFECT STORM
### October 31, 1991

Several climatic conditions aligned together to form what the *National Weather Service* called, **"The Perfect Storm."** Though storms in the North Atlantic usually move from west to east, this unusual storm tracked in the *opposite* direction from east to west. This storm was immortalized by the book, *Perfect Storm*, by Sebastian Junger and made into a popular movie. One of the first places this storm hit was Kennebunkport, Maine. Waves over 30 feet caused damage to hundreds of homes including severe damage to the home of George H. Bush. Waves 10-30 feet high were common from North Carolina to Maine during this phenomenal storm. Ocean City, Maryland recorded the highest tide ever at nearly 8 feet![2]

---

## OSLO/ HURRICANE ANDREW-
August 23, 1992

One year later, President Bush was meeting in Washington, D.C. in order to re-ignite the idea of *land for peace*. **On the very same day, August 23, 1992, the WORST NATURAL DISASTER TO EVER HIT THE UNITED STATES** bore down on Florida in the form of Hurricane Andrew. 180,000 homes were destroyed and over 30 billion in losses were due to this storm that would soon be outdone by one record-breaking disaster after another.[3]

## PICKING UP THE PIECES-
January 16

On the 16th of January 1994, then President Clinton under political pressure to do something about the Middle East unrest, met with Syria's President Hafez-el-Assad in Geneva. They entertained the thought of Israel giving up the *Golan Heights*, a strategic mountain range historically owned by Israel and captured from the Syrians in the 1967- 6-day war. **IN LESS THAN 24 HOURS,** a powerful 6.9 earthquake hit an urban center in Southern California, a suburb of Los Angeles causing 57 deaths and over 20 billion in losses. This was noted to be the **costliest earthquake disaster in U.S. history.** [4]

## ISRAEL GIVES BACK LAND

*On May 14, 1948, the first day of Israel's existence as a nation since Roman days, Egypt, Syria, Jordan, and other Arab states attacked Israel for the purpose of destroying it.*

*In 1967, Egypt and Syria invaded Israel again for the same purpose, and it was then that the West Bank, Jerusalem, and Golan Heights were taken back into Israel's possession. Israel captured the Sinai Peninsula in this war and having no desire for land that does not rightly belong to them,* ***promptly returned it back to Egypt.***

**FINANCIAL PEACE:** November 30, 1998

_____

The leader of the Palestinians, Chairman Yasser Arafat arrived in Washington on **November 30, 1998** to meet with President Bill Clinton to raise money for a Palestinian state with Jerusalem as its capital. With America promising 400 million and the European nations 1.7 billion, **THE VERY SAME DAY**, **November 30,** the European Market had its worst day in history. Hundreds of billions of dollars were wiped away both in the European and U.S. Stock Markets. [5]

## PERSONAL PEACE

President Clinton arrived in Israel on **December 12, 1998** to discuss another *land for peace* deal. **ON THE SAME DAY, December 12,** the Congress of the United States voted four *articles of impeachment* against the President.

## RECORD-BREAKING PEACE

---

On May 3, 1999, emboldened by Clinton who praised him for "his aspirations for his own land," Yasser Arafat scheduled a press conference to announce a *"Palestinian State"*, with Jerusalem as its capital. **ON THAT DAY**, THE MOST POWERFUL TORNADO STORM SYSTEM TO EVER HIT THE UNITED STATES HIT THE MIDSECTION IN OKLAHOMA AND KANSAS WITH WINDS CLOCKED AT **RECORD-BREAKING 316 MILES PER HOUR**, THE FASTEST WIND SPEED EVER RECORDED! [6]

**At first, I could not understand why the leaders of this country did not personally bear the brunt of disbelieving and disobeying God's promises concerning Israel until I realized that we are a** *representative government* **and whatever our leaders do in office, we are ultimately responsible because we chose them to represent us.**

**An alarm is being sounded that the matters described in this book can be no coincidence. The odds would be so great as to be beyond belief. There must be a plan, an** *"X-Factor"* **that we are missing. I shall**

later explain what is meant by this special factor and the reason these matters are of such vital interest to the One who created all things for His glory! So no matter what political party we subscribe to, if we truly want this country to remain blessed, we must vote for those who have a heart for Israel in action and not in word only! Other important matters, economy, moral issues, defense... are all secondary if we are to fulfill our role as a useful and free nation upon the earth.

## TWIN TOWERS 9-11-2001

In August of 2001, George W. Bush went on *CNN* and demanded that Arafat stop terrorism in order to bring Israel to the negotiating table. Shortly after, the Saudi's threatened to withhold oil from the United States if something wasn't done about Middle East peace. As a result, Bush declared that the Palestinians have a right to their own state and homeland, in essence rewarding the Saudi's for their behavior.

A deadline was fixed for a Palestinian state in Israel by 2005 and the U.S. Ambassador to Saudi Arabia and his team worked on the official documents. These documents meant to partition part of Israel's land, were finalized by the ambassador's office and sent to the President's office on the eve of the *Terror Attacks* of September 11, 2001! [7]

'O JERUSALEM,
JERUSALEM...HOW OFTEN I
WOULD HAVE GATHERED
YOUR CHILDREN TOGETHER,
EVEN AS A HEN GATHERS HER
CHICKS UNDER HER WINGS
AND YOU WOULD NOT!'

-Luke 13:34

# CHAPTER I

# "O JERUSALEM, JERUSALEM"

Jerusalem is a city of historical and infinite significance. The latter part of the name, "Jeru-salem," derives from the Hebrew word, *"shalom,"* meaning *prosperity, divine favor, healing, and peace.* David chose to make Jerusalem his home over three thousand years ago and the city will forever be known as the *"City of David!"*

Jerusalem is more than magical; it is a city of majesty and of huge spiritual relevance! It is an eternal city and the destiny of all mankind will forever be linked to this city set on a hill known as **Mount Zion!**

There is no foreign policy that has more direct and profound implications on the economy and health of our nation as does our policy toward Israel.

A better understanding of Israel's humble beginnings will help to explain why *Jerusalem* has and always will be the center and capital of Israel.

## DAVID 1000 B.C.

The thought of *forgetting* Jerusalem was the reason that one of Israel's most prominent kings pronounced a conditional curse upon himself! King David penned these words some 3000 years ago...

*..."O Jerusalem, If I forget thee, may my right hand forget its skill...if I prefer not Jerusalem above my chief joy" (Psalm 137:5).*

David, Israel's beloved poet and musician would be devastated if unable ever to play his instrument or fight in another battle. It was his music that caused his promotion from the Judean sheepfolds to the palace in Israel. His skill of playing songs soothed and brought comfort to Israel's first king, Saul.

He was willing to risk it all for the love of *Jerusalem!* What is it about Jerusalem that was so important to his memory and why is it still considered to be the *joy of the whole earth*?

My interest on this subject began in August of 2005 while witnessing images of 8500 Jewish families being removed from their beloved homeland in the Gaza Strip.

The displacing of entire communities began simultaneously with the eye of Hurricane Katrina taking dead aim at my hometown New Orleans! I told my wife that these events seem eerily connected and so I began to write down dates with coinciding events and decided to publish these amazing findings.

*Calamities* that have befallen our nation over the last decade reveal a disturbing trend. *Our elected officials were busy placing untoward political pressure upon Israel to surrender parts of her homeland!* **If a pattern or design exists, then there must be a designer behind it!** This is no indictment on any particular leader or administration, but rather to show that the voters themselves in a representative democracy are the culpable party.

## ISRAEL'S BEGINNING

Thousands of years before the founding of America, a nation was forming through the faith and obedience of one man, Abram who dwelt in the land of the Chaldeans (modern-day Iraq). This relationship was initiated by God who required good-faith from His new friend. Abram believed that God was able to keep His promise.

*"Now the Lord said to Abram, 'Get thee out of thy country, and from thy kindred, and from thy father's house, unto a **land** that I will show thee (Genesis 12:1). {Emphasis mine}*

His name was later changed from Abram to Abraham as a result of his covenant relationship with God. It was common to take the name of the party one entered into covenant with. Hence, God's name was inserted to the middle of his name forming the "Ah" sound of YHWH, a name of God.

## ISRAEL'S HISTORY

*Israel* has an unparalleled history in importance and longevity. It is a *small parcel* of land in the Middle East- no wider than one hour drive from east to west and no longer than a mere 3.5 mile drive from north to south. The Mediterranean Sea is the western border with Jordan to the east and Egypt to the south.

Size can be deceiving since Israel has the largest natural deposits of minerals on the planet. Take all the mineral sources on earth, *combine them all together,* and they will not equal the vast wealth contained at the bottom of Israel's *Dead Sea.*

**"*The Land of Promise,*" another name for Israel, is vital to the history as well as the future of all mankind. The promise, though beginning with Abram, was to be the hope of the entire world!**

*"...And in thee shall all the families of the earth be blessed" (Genesis 12:3b).*

This is the land of the people that witnessed the promised messiah, Jesus of Nazareth enter her gates humbly riding upon a donkey, the foal of a colt. All of Christendom has its hope in the transaction purchased by Christ by his sacrificial offering outside of these gates.

Mountain Olive View of Eastern Gate

## ZION IS LINKED WITH JERUSALEM [1]

Zion is inseparably linked with the city of Jerusalem. David's capital city of Jerusalem was located on *Mount Zion*. It was on this mountain that Abraham offered his son Isaac and the place where Solomon built the *First Temple*. Returning exiles under the leadership of Ezra and Nehemiah rebuilt the Temple on the exact location that had been destroyed by the Babylonians in 586 B.C..

The name "*Zion*" suddenly appears on the biblical scene in 1000 B.C. when David captured the Jebusite fortress on the southern ridge of Mount Zion.

*"Nevertheless David took the stronghold of Zion; the same is the city of David" (2 Samuel 5:7; cf.*
*1 Chronicles 11:5).*

The city was originally called Salem then the Jebusites renamed it Jebus. Under David's leadership, the city came to be known as Jerusalem. The Lord's choosing of this mountain to make His home is what makes this city the most unique of all locations on earth.

*"Sing praises to the Lord who dwells in Zion" (Psalm 9:11).*

*"For the Lord has chosen Zion; he has desired it for his habitation...This is my rest forever..." (Psalm 132:13-14).*

## AN EARLIER PRIESTHOOD

God's interest in this intriguing land can be seen over a thousand years before King David. After defeating 5 kings that had kidnapped his nephew, Lot, Abraham was met by a Priest who had an eternal ministry. There was no recorded beginning to this priest Melchizedek, nor a recorded ending. Because the first Jewish priesthood was insufficient under Moses and Aaron to finally take away the sins of the nations, God promised he would make a new covenant with the nation and this of course would require another priesthood.  (Please read Jeremiah 31:31) We can see from the writer of the book of Hebrews, that this new High Priest, no less than God's own Son would forever be a priest after a different order than Aaron.  His priesthood would be after the order of AN UNCHANGING PRIESTHOOD, after Melchizedek's Order.

EVEN THOUGH THE COVENANT WITH MAN WOULD CHANGE ALONG WITH AN ETERNAL PRIESTHOOD, ONE THING REMAINS THE SAME- JERUSALEM IS THE ETERNAL CAPITAL AND DWELLING WHERE GOD WILL ONE DAY RULE FOREVER. Never has God discussed any changes in His desire for JERUSALEM!

Kevin Howard points out in his excellent
article, *"The Location of the Temple,"* that not
only had God chosen Zion (Jerusalem) to be
his resting place forever but that he used
David as his representative to actually legally
purchase the land. He says, **"Like any other
real estate dispute, ownership of the
Temple Mount must be legally resolved
based upon the historical transfer of its
title deed. Mount Zion was legally
purchased 3,000 years ago by King David
for the location of the Holy Temple. This
occurred sixteen hundred years *before* the
time of Mohammed, long before any
controversy existed. This was the last
transfer of title.**

The property was not taken by force, it
was not stolen. It was not received as a gift.
It was not obtained at a discount. David paid
full market value for this property. He
obtained a legal, clear title deed to the
Temple Mount. As the legal representation
for the nation of Israel, David purchased
Mount Zion for the Lord (2Samuel 24:18-19;
24-25). This property was then placed under

the custodianship of the Jewish people for the Temple of the Lord."

I really like this part. He goes on to say, "The transfer of title was not lost. The historical record of the occasion, the physical location, the terms, and the sale price of the property still exists today. God's Word carefully documented these details as critical legal history of the Holy Temple. The record of Mount Zion's purchase is translated into more than one hundred languages, contained in hundreds of millions of copies of the Bible, and located in countless homes, hotel rooms, and places of worship around the planet. The ownership of Zion is substantiated by *the most documented title abstract in history."*

David's passion for Jerusalem is well documented. He was a king who ruled for 40 years over Israel and was renowned for his fighting skills and love of music. He built his house and palace in what was later to become known as David's stronghold, Zion, the city of the great king! He is also credited with making this city the center of national worship when he erected a tent and allowed everyone to enter the presence of God with music, singing, and rejoicing! This was truly revolutionary for since the time of Moses, only the priests were allowed to enter the structure to minister to the Lord and only one priest was allowed for one day out of the entire year!  This tent came to be known as *"The Tabernacle of David."*

## DAVID ESTABLISHES WORSHIP IN ZION

The very first act David performed when he was installed as king of Israel was to bring the Ark of the Covenant, which had been captured by the Philistines, back to its home, Jerusalem!  The Ark represented the very *presence* of God.

Moses had been given instructions to build this rectangular shaped chest inlaid and overlaid with gold.  Its contents would include a golden pot of manna as a reminder of God's provisions for them during their exodus from Egypt.  Another article included in this chest was an almond staff that actually produced live buds, a supernatural occurrence God used to endorse Aaron's priesthood under Moses.  Also, it would contain the two stone tablets upon which the Ten Commandments were written.  Finally, two worshipping angels made of pure gold were crafted above the Ark facing one another in a posture of worship.  God's presence in the form of a cloud dwelt between the two angels above the Ark known as the Mercy Seat.

As long as the Philistines had the Ark of the Covenant in their possession, untold misery came upon them! Upon realizing they were suffering as a result of having this strange rectangle-shaped box in their possession, they sought for a way to return it! *Notice one nation's curse is another nation's blessing!* We are suffering as a result of offending God's presence and as David did, let's make it our priority to seek for His glorious return! I'm not saying God has left America, but there is a point where constant offences can result in a lifting of His care and provision. It's not too late to pray for God to visit our nation once again and leave behind a blessing!

As long as the Ark was in the possession of Israel, they prospered and could not be defeated. David was anxious to recover what had been stolen by the Philistines as a result of a priest named Eli. He refused to correct his out-of-control and irreverent sons who preyed upon the young women at the gate of the temple and kept the best offerings for themselves.

The pomp and circumstance of its return is all recorded in the official "*Chronicles of the Kings*." You can read the details of David's trials and heartaches as he struggled to complete the home-coming of this holy element that represented the *very presence and glory of God.*

At first, David forgot to consult the Law of Moses in order to transport the *Ark* according to divine specification. Death and destruction ensued when one of the cart drivers reached out to steady the special box after hitting a bump. Immediately the man was killed. David became discouraged and stopped the transfer until he figured out the proper method of travel. Instead of riding the Ark upon a hand-made cart, he instead properly appointed priests that would use staves and carry the Ark without ever actually having to handle it.

Never has the nation of Israel known such joy and peace as when their leader humbled himself and personally led the procession for its glorious return! The Ark of the Covenant was the central component to Israel's worship of the One True God, and its home was Jerusalem!

## A HEART FOR JERUSALEM

Jesus was **broken-hearted** over Jerusalem. We should all take note of the things that breaks God's heart! This is considered *"The beginning of all wisdom."*

For many centuries God had sent prophets to the children of Israel after they would wander from His commandments. Many of them were tortured, imprisoned, and even killed. Jesus would experience the same rejection and humiliation at the hands of their ancestors. His message to them was the same as the others, "Repent and return to the One who loves you and redeemed you!" God's love for Abraham's children has never once waned or diminished.

Zion was supposed to be the mountain where all nations would gather to worship the King, the Creator of the heavens and the earth who had revealed Himself. *How could that city, dedicated to worshipping the One True God, shut their ears and close their eyes in the time of their visitation?*

## JERUSALEM TODAY

Jerusalem is a holy place to Muslims, Christians and Jews but only the Jews can claim rights to it. God promised this land to Abraham and declared it in writing in a legal document called the Bible along with a complete survey of the land with boundaries including the Mediterranean Sea to the East and Egypt to the south.

*"If earth is the center of the universe,
Jerusalem is the center of the earth!"*
E.W. Kenyon [4]

## GOD HAS CHOSEN JERUSALEM

Without the city of Jerusalem, the state of
Israel could not exist. Jerusalem is the heart
and soul of *Zionism*.

It is now and will be the center of the
universe! A sort of *heaven on earth*! There
will be no world peace till there is peace in
Jerusalem. There is no other city on earth
that can compare to it because it is nothing
less than the '*City of God*.'[5]

*I (God) have chosen Jerusalem that my
name might be there.... For now I have
chosen and sanctified this house [the temple],
that my name might be there forever; and My
eyes and My heart may be there
perpetually....In this house and in Jerusalem,
which I have chosen, will I place My name
forever (II Chronicles 6:6, 7:16, 33:7).*

God's presence dwells in Jerusalem. I
have visited this city and have traveled to

several spectacular places in the world but the feeling I received in Jerusalem is like no other! Friends have relayed their experiences to me how they crossed into Egypt once during a tour of the Middle East. When they crossed the border into Egypt, they could feel a heavy feeling of oppression. As soon as they crossed back into Israel, it lifted and the beautiful presence of God returned!

Jerusalem's significance cannot be overstated. It was the place that Solomon, the son of David built the *First Temple* of worship to the God of Israel! Today it is known as one of the *Seven Wonders of the World.*

## PROSPERITY PRAYING

Many are looking for success in life. Not long ago, I happened upon Jabez's prayer while reading scripture. I noticed that his simple prayer was accepted by God. It was on that day I decided that if God was pleased with Jabez's prayer, surely he would hear mine as well. His prayer consisted of three parts. The first was, *"God, bless me indeed!"* The second was, *"Enlarge my coast,"* I trusted it would work for me even though I happen to live in the mountains and not a coastal city like Israel. The third part of his prayer was, *"Let your hand be with me so that my soul is not grieved by the evil in this world."*

I have found God's favor upon my family as I diligently pray each day for these *three things*.

But there is another divine key to prayer I would like to share with you. This involves stretching yourself to pray for a land you may have never visited and are not very familiar with. One little known secret is that God promises to prosper those who will pray for the peace of Jerusalem. Think of it, pray for peace to come to the *"City of Peace."* No wonder trouble comes to those who seek to separate and divide this **prayer-soaked** city! If only her neighbors would accept the gift of land offered. Peace would then be guaranteed for both.

*"Pray for the peace of Jerusalem:* ***They shall prosper that love thee"*** *(Psalm 122:6).*

It is interesting that God would call people who pray to remember to pray for Jerusalem! There is no other city that God asks us to intercede for and it comes with a tremendous reward.

As is the reward, so is the warning concerning this treasured land. God makes clear that anyone who touches (harms) Israel and *Jerusalem* in particular touches the apple of His eye. In other words it brings irritation much like you would be irritated if someone stuck their finger in your eye*!*

*Which brings us back to the purpose for this book: To uncover the importance of having godly leaders in office that will have it right concerning Israel. It should come as no surprise that she just happens to be our only true friend and ally in the entire Middle East!*

It isn't enough to elect someone due to their religious affiliation! As mentioned earlier, Christian leaders can have strong religious convictions but don't understand the Biblical status of the Jewish nation. Many believe that God has finished His dealings with the Jews, and therefore he is justified to help divide up their property for the promise of peace. We must always vote for the one who supports Israel.

It also isn't even enough to just vote a Jewish person into office. Many Jews are not well versed in the promises and covenants of God and can actually cause more harm than good if elected simply on the basis of heritage. We cannot forget the legacy of *Isaac Rabin* and *Ariel Sharon*, two leaders in Israel who partnered with those who would bargain Israel's security for a temporary truce. Their complicity in this matter will be discussed in the following chapter.

---

---

# 'WHAT *YOU* MEANT FOR EVIL, *GOD* HAS MEANT FOR GOOD,'

JOSEPH

−Genesis 50:20

---

# CHAPTER II

# POLITICAL ABOMINATION

There is a reason for many of the troubles America is facing. We have lost our way and we are receiving correction just as a good parent would correct the son or daughter he/she loves. Chastening seems unbearable at times but it always yields the fruit of peace and maturity.

Abomination derives from an ancient biblical word meaning: *"A loathsome act or thing."*[1] When an act has been egregiously or flagrantly committed, we would say that an "*abominable act*" has been perpetrated. In a court of law the most severe penalties are handed out when the judge or jury determines that the suspect has committed *a disgusting act*.

The disasters that our nation has suffered in recent history can only be interpreted in the light of God's passion for Jerusalem! **How else can so many disastrous events be** determined against our homeland on the exact day or within 24 hours of demands placed upon Israel to give up land?

## GOD'S FIRST LOVE WAS ISRAEL

Some may feel like God has abandoned His people due to His personal dealings with them, but this is not the case! God's relationship with Israel is like a married couple much in love that has been separated for a very long time and is being joined back once again in marriage. This is a most joyous moment in history for Israel and the Jewish people as a whole do not even realize it! God has a fondness for the Jew and describes them as the *twinkle in His eye*. **We as a nation must be careful how we treat Israel!**

When you read the following passage, you will notice that many centuries ago the city of Jerusalem had fallen into ruins and the boundary lines had become blurred; but a man was sent to survey the land and replace the landmarks to their original locations. Keep in mind that this was a time the land was barren, and except for a small remnant of folks, it was mostly uninhabitable.

*"... and I looked and behold a man with a measuring line in his hand...measuring Jerusalem. Jerusalem shall be inhabited with the multitude of men and of cattle. For he that touches you touches the apple of God's eye. The Lord... has chosen Jerusalem."* (Zechariah 2: vss.1, 2,8,12).

We should once again consider C.S Spurgeon's words pertaining to nations and kingdoms. ***"There is a judgment also passing upon nations, for as nations will not exist as nations in another world, they have to be judged and punished in this present state."*** He begs the question concerning formidable empires and kingdoms, ***"Where are they today?" One need only do a casual study of the greatest world empires such as Babylon, Persia, Rome, to see that they were violently overthrown and that the world is much better off without them!***[2]

The purpose of this book is to awaken our citizens to the spiritual ramifications that exist in our state and federal elections. We have overcome and prevailed over many and various adversities in our short history but how will we prevail and continue to exist if we make an enemy of God?

---

We should be familiar with *"The Roadmap to Peace,"* in order to understand that it is flawed. It requires Israel to give up its inheritance including East Jerusalem and the international prayer destination known as the *"Wailing Wall."* This document also demands Israel to comply at her own peril.

Wailing Wall

It would be a travesty for Israel's leaders to side with the majority and allow its own land to be taken away for the fleeting promise of peace.

Recent Israeli leaders willing to relinquish parts of Jerusalem were met with extremely unfortunate fates:

**Isaac Rabin** was the first native born Prime Minister of Israel. While in office, he signed the *Oslo Accord* and was willing to trade land for peace. He served two terms, 1974-1977 and 1992 until his assassination in 1995.[3]

**Ariel Sharon** was an army officer in the Israeli army since its inception in 1948. He participated in the *"1948 War of Independence"*, *"The Qibya Massacre of 1953"*, the *"1956 Suez War"*, the *"Six-day War of 1967"*, and the *"Yom Kippur War of 1973"*. He served as Israel's Prime Minister from 2001-2006 and championed Israeli settlements in the West Bank and Gaza. However, he orchestrated Israel's unilateral disengagement from the Gaza Strip beginning in 2005 and in January 2006, he suffered a stroke leaving him in a vegetative state.[4]

Disasters have increased dramatically in the United States since the beginning of 2011 when the final phase of the roadmap was publicly declared and endorsed by the Obama administration. This final phase includes the ceding of East Jerusalem over to the

Palestinians in exchange for *peace*. As a woman's labor pains increase nearing the time of delivery, the United States has seen more frequent storms and natural disasters. Ironically, heavily populated cities were visited with record breaking devastation.

**Things began to intensify in the United States when it was announced that Jerusalem does not belong to Israel.** It wasn't till we began to touch the natural capital of Israel, Jerusalem that we began to see cracks 1 ¼ inch wide and indefinite closure of the *Washington Monument* in Washington, D.C.![5]

Another example of this is the Tuscaloosa, Alabama tornado that struck in April of 2011. Though it did not strike the University of Alabama, destruction and devastation came to the city that hosts this legendary campus.

Still another was the Joplin, Missouri tornado that took a literal direct route straight down *"Main Street,"* obliterating all emergency services including police headquarters and main hospital. I still remember the news media describing the tornado splitting the city into two.

Another major water event, *Hurricane Irene* came only days after President Barrack

Obama called on Israel to apologize to Turkey. Israel was blamed for infractions due to the *Turkish Flotilla* that illegally entered Israeli territorial waterways in the summer of 2011. Israel's soldiers did not react upon entering the violating vessels until their lives were threatened with deadly force.

While on vacation, the President issued a threat to Israeli leaders to, *"Apologize to Turkey, or else!"*[6] Hurricane Irene struck during this time and brought heavy flooding to the east coast and particularly the northeast where the President had to shorten his family vacation at Martha's Vineyard. It didn't take long for the one doing the threatening to himself feel the threat of a violent force of nature.

## ALL ROADS LEAD TO JERUSALEM

So the road that was supposed to lead to peace in the Middle East took the final curve upward to Jerusalem in the *spring of 2011*. The Palestinian resolve to secure her as a capital city came plainly into view and the Obama administration became adamant that Jerusalem must be placed upon the

---

[6]

negotiating table in order to restart stalled peace talks.

As a nation, we must ask ourselves the question, "What we are doing wrong that is causing such calamity?" Instead of divine guidance, provision, and protection that we have enjoyed in our past, we are experiencing calamities and economic hardship. **In January through September 2011, ten events totaling over 35 billion in losses** have struck our shores and we still have yet another four months to go![7] This does not take into account the enormous loss of life. The amazing thing is each of these storms have one and only one common denominator, *we were busy turning our back on our friend and ally, Israel!*

My sacred advice to the readers who love this country is to diligently give an attentive ear to the political debates and especially when the subject of Israel is discussed. Trust me, it will be discussed for it is the primary reason this nation has changed in such a short amount of time! There is no bias within these pages toward any political party or elected officials in the following corresponding events. None of the dates are contrived but documented and sources named for your own investigative purposes.   Most of this information can be found online in official government websites or news archives.

We all have an agenda that we subscribe too and that is our freedom but we must place them second to the security and protection of Israel.   If we want to remain a nation under God, we must prioritize accordingly.   **"Am I my brothers' keeper?"**   Cain asked this about his brother and the right answer of course is **YES!**   We also have the distinct benefit of calling Israel our closest friend in the entire Middle East.

The *"Quartet's"* road map was seriously flawed due to their disregard for the ancient landmarks.   Fortunately, there is still time to turn this nation back to being *"One Nation under God."* This can only be accomplished by voting for those who respect the history of Israel and her direct relationship with the God who has blessed America.   We can't claim to be under God if we continue to do things that disgust Him.   We do so at our own peril, so let's vote for those who are true friends to Israel.   It is vital to help those get elected who still believe that God has a purpose for America!   Other issues are important as well, but we do well to remember that our future depends on getting this issue right!

This book is about **hope** and **future**. Just as there could not have been a modern Israel without a *Holocaust*, so things cannot get better for America till we experience meaningful hardships. **Things are about to get better! Things are about to change!**

'THERE IS A WAY THAT
SEEMS RIGHT UNTO A
MAN, BUT THE END
THEREOF ARE THE WAYS
OF DEATH.'

**KING SOLOMON**
**-Proverbs 16:25 KJV**

# CHAPTER III

# ' THE ROAD TO HELL'

Over thirty years ago, I borrowed a book from my wife's uncle Billy, documenting the "*1967 6-Day War*" in Israel. It was fought in only 6 days and began with several Arab neighbor-states attacking Israel simultaneously. I was struck by the voracity of Israel's defense of their homeland in disabling the air forces of each of those nations on the morning of the first day! Also, there were reports of Arab soldiers laying down their weapons in surrender even though they had greatly outnumbered Israeli forces. When asked why they refused to fight, their response was that they saw visions and rather large figures fighting on the side with Israel.

One report tells of a **swarm of hornets attacking a Jordanian Tank Force,** causing them to stop their tanks and flee in terror.

In another account, **six Israeli soldiers captured 300 Egyptian soldiers**. When asked why they surrendered, the Egyptian Fighters told of **seeing large angels in white shining apparel with flaming swords,** standing behind the Israelis.

God promised Moses that He would send His Angel to lead them and He would also **employ hornets to drive out their enemies** so they could possess the land of Canaan. (Exodus 23:28; 33:2; Deuteronomy 7:20). (Max Solbrekken,D.D)

Lands that legitimately belonged to the attacking nations were promptly restored back to them.

One day, upon visiting Uncle Billy and realizing I had kept his book for an inordinate amount of time, I informed him that I meant to return the book with each visit but regretfully forgot. I will never forget his kind and gracious response to me with that infectious smile of his, *'The road to hell is paved with good intentions."* Uncle Billy was an insurance executive, and I've often wondered how many times he used that line while trying to sell *a life policy.* Well, I soon returned the book and Uncle Billy taught me a valuable life-lesson, that is; *intentions even though well meaning are not quite good enough!*

## YESHA LEADERS

Leaders such as George W. Bush, Barrack Obama, Colin Powell, Bill Clinton, to name a few, are well intentioned men, but navigating peace in the Middle East is not done without careful historical studies of the ancient boundaries and inheritance documents.

In a letter recently written to U.N. Secretary-General Ban Ki-Moon, men known as Yesha Leaders (i.e. members of a council that oversees Jewish settlements in the West Bank and Gaza Strip),explained that the Bible, the Quran, and international agreements document Israel to be the land of the Jewish People. Citing the Bible as *"Recording for all time the awarding of the Land of Israel to the forefathers of the Jewish People by the Creator of the world,"* the letter asks him to correct the deviations of nations in accordance with international law.

They also write, *"The entire Land of Israel was promised and granted to the Jewish People...as recorded time and again in the opening five books of the Hebrew Bible,(e.g. Genesis 15: 21; Deuteronomy 1:8), accepted by adherents of the Christian faith whose Bible encompasses the aforementioned Books, and confirmed in various places in the book of Islam, the Quran, (Sura2)."*

The letter concludes with the following statement, *"The time has undoubtedly come-in fact is long overdue Mr. Secretary-General, for the international community as represented by the U.N. to recognize the fact that the Arabs of the Land of Israel do not want their own state, nor do they want to conclude a peace treaty with the State of Israel; all they desire is the destruction of Israel. The time has indeed come to reaffirm international recognition of the immutable rights of the Jewish People to all of their historical homeland."*[1]

## ROAD MAP

The sponsors of the road map known as *"The Quartet"* include the United States, the European Union, Russia, and the United Nations. The principles of the plan were first outlined by our U.S. president in a speech given on June 24, 2002 in which he called for an independent Palestinian state living side by side with its neighbor Israel in peace. The goal was to end the conflict by 2005 and included three separate phases:

**Phase 1** included the Israeli withdrawal from Gaza.

**Phase 2** would include the evacuation from the West Bank.

**Phase 3** was to sort out the *"Jerusalem"* issue, with the Palestinians seeking to divide the city and set up its capital in the eastern sector.[2]

The first step on the road map was for the Palestinians to elect its first ever Prime Minister and Mahmoud Abbas was selected. President Bush visited the Middle East in June of 2003 attending two summits to try and push the plan along. During this time, Israel released 100 Palestinian prisoners in a gesture of good faith. Israel insisted that known terrorists who had Israeli blood on their hands would not be released.

Soon after he left the region, the Palestinians launched a series of attacks threatening to derail the peace process. With a tentative truce at the end of the month and with several deaths on both sides it became clear that the 2005 deadline would not be reached.

On May 24, 2005, in his joint press conference with Palestinian Leader Abbas, our president pushed for the removal of Israeli settlers from so-called Palestinian territories. He made it clear that this is the final position of the United States till the conclusion of the plan.

## TRADING LAND FOR LAND

Many felt this was biased toward Palestinians. In *August*, the Israelis began to implement the withdrawal, but something unusual was beginning to stir in the Gulf of Mexico at the exact same hour!

I shall never forget the news images I watched of Jewish families being torn from their houses and land by Israeli Security forces. The images blasted all over the world were horrifying and I feared for our national culpability in this heart wrenching evil.

*At the same time*, I was switching channels to follow the worst hurricane I'd ever witnessed filling the Gulf of Mexico with an eye that looked angry, vindictive, and full of purpose. I told my wife that this is a direct result of our demands on Israel to dislodge Jewish settlers from their homes in Gaza and *bulldoze* their properties.

*"Vengeance is mine, saith the Lord, I will repay." (Romans 12:9)*

Here is an account from NHB Christian Talks Ministry of the parallel events:

*During the month of August 2005, with pressure from the US, the dreaded D-Day came. Over 8500 begging Jewish settlers were forcibly removed from the Gaza Strip. I watched in unbelief as the Jewish people were crying and pleading to remain in their homes and land. The Israeli soldiers came and literally dragged them from their houses. At the orders of the U.S. and against the protests of the Israeli Government, bulldozers came and demolished their homes. The land was given to terrorists who celebrated and shouted, "Death to Israel!"*

*As soon as the debacle was over, Condoleeza Rice began urging Israel to vacate the West Bank. This would be considered Phase II of Phase III.*

*August 23- the SAME DAY- Tropical Storm Katrina appeared below the Bahamas with meteorologists claiming no need to fear this low-impact storm. Defying the computer models, Katrina turned southeast and with a vengeance took dead aim at the houses and land of S. Louisiana and Mississippi. Beautiful homes were left as piles of worthless rubble as if someone bulldozed them. Over 10 thousand dead and an estimated final bill of 150 billion, along with hundreds of thousands left homeless."[3]*

---

## KATRINA

Upon realizing that New Orleans would take a direct hit and the mayor ordering mandatory evacuations calling Katrina, "The mother of all storms," my attention turned away from the heart-break of Jewish mothers, fathers, and children. **GOD WAS NOT DISTRACTED!** While Jews were displaced, a storm seemed prepared to displace our own residents from their homes.

Katrina made its second landfall at the Gulf Coast on the morning of August 29, 2005. Eighty percent of the city of New Orleans was flooded along with neighboring parishes and due to breeches in two separate levee systems, the water remained for weeks.

**TIMELINE**: Katrina formed over Bahamas as a **Category 1** storm on **August 23** before crossing south Florida. It would eventually become a **Category 3** before hitting the Louisiana and Mississippi gulf coasts.

Mandatory evacuations of Jews from the northern West Bank and Gaza along with the demolition of properties began on **August 15 and would continue for several weeks. IT WAS AT THE HEIGHT OF THESE EVICTIONS THAT KATRINA STRUCK!**

# HURRICANE RITA: MORE DEVAS-
# TATING THAN KATRINA

The eviction and dismantling of Jewish settlers and their properties from the West Bank by Israel Security Forces was to be completed by *September 22, 2005*. On *September 23*, the **Category 5 Hurricane Rita** struck on the Sabine Pass of Texas/ Louisiana border.  Rita was the **4th largest hurricane ever recorded** in the Gulf of Mexico and caused 11.5 billion in damage entirely destroying some coastal communities.[4]

Due to *Katrina*, little attention was paid to the devastating impact this storm made on the nation's economy.  This storm came and reeked havoc with the oil fields and refineries off the Texas and Louisiana coasts.  The gas prices skyrocketed along with predictions that the earth was running out of oil.  Saudi Arabia would never verify these false claims nor would they refute them.  Only silence. **Gas prices have never retreated to pre-Rita levels!**

---

## GALVESTON FOR GAZA

On August 19, 2009, just three months after Congress urged President Obama to end violence in Gaza, a hurricane would form off the coast of Africa and make its way to the city of Galveston, Texas. A thousand rockets were fired into southern Israel but Israel was once again pressured to leave her own land. It was during this time of America influenced Israeli duress that an under-reported storm raked the Texas coast.

*Hurricane Ike* would make its devastating landfall on September 13. It would be the 3rd costliest storm in American history! Yes, **GALVESTON FOR GAZA**. It is not known how many people were literally washed out to sea, and we may never know. A twelve foot surge brought seventeen foot waves that topped the seawall facing the Gulf of Mexico. Before the eye passed over Houston, eight feet of water flooded the airport and downtown Galveston was submerged with over 6 feet of water in the courthouse.[5]

---

# LOUISIANA- GULF OIL SPILL
## APRIL 20, 2010

The Christian Science Monitor[6] reported that on the **_WEEK-END of APRIL 20-21 of 2010,_** the Israeli Government rejected Obama's calls for a halt to building in East Jerusalem. This call was rejected by Netanyahu and approval was given to build 1600 residences on the part of Jerusalem captured from Jordan in the 1967, 6-day war. **_ON THE VERY SAME WEEKEND, APRIL 20,2010,_** an explosion of Deepwater Horizon took the lives of 11 men and spilt nearly 5 million barrels of crude oil into the Gulf of Mexico, ravaging the wildlife, fragile wetlands, and vital seafood industries of the Gulf Coast.

## RECORDHOME FORECLOSURES- 2010

In the same year that America was demanding a stop order to the building of houses and condo's in East Jerusalem, America itself saw a record of nearly 4 million foreclosures on properties filed by banks around the country.[7]

All of these national disasters came as a result of only the first 2 of 3 phases of this failed peace policy. **THE *REAL BATTLE* IS AND ALWAYS HAS BEEN FOR THE HEART AND SOUL OF JERUSALEM!**

# 'VEANGENCE IS MINE SAITH THE LORD, I WILL REPAY.'

- ROMANS 12:19

# CHAPTER IV

# THE *FINAL* PHASE BEGINS.

## THE ARAB SPRING 2011

The spring of 2011 came to be known as the "*Arab Spring*" when opposition groups in the Middle East, beginning with Tunisia, began to overthrow their dictators and cast off decades of oppressive regimes. The spring also became the starting point of **Phase 3** with the United States placing **East Jerusalem** on the table as a pre-condition for new peace talks between the Israelis and Palestinians. A demand was made on Israel by the Obama administration to return to pre-1967 indefensible borders once again as a pre-condition to restarting talks. I visited Israel in 2000 and walked upon the Golan Heights captured from Syria in 1967. I can tell you, whoever controls that expansive mountain range has direct rocket and missile access to Galilee and surrounding cities

*THIS IS WHERE HISTORY HAS IT WRONG IM0. You may ask, what do you mean by that. The proper name for this period in history should have been and forever will be* **THE JERUSALEM SPRING!**

**There can be no coincidence once again that the whole of the Middle-East was set on fire at the same time we called for Jerusalem TO BE DIVIDED. The Palestinians must have a capital for their homeland and the United States at the time of this writing still doesn't recognize Jerusalem as Israel's capital. As Arabs over the region sought to overthrow their dictators, our leaders found themselves on the wrong side of the conflict. The Muslim Brotherhood, a notorious Islamist group with ties to Hamas was backed by President Obama after repeated warnings from Israeli leaders and many experts in the area of foreign relations.**

We shouldn't be fooled by the term, Arab Spring, for this was the beginning for the battle over Jerusalem and the proper leaders for the Arab States seemingly had become too complacent for it to happen.

## JERUSALEM FACTOR 2011

In March of 2011, President Obama hosted a meeting with the Prime Minister of Israel, Benjamin Netanyahu. After failing to extract a written promise of concessions on settlements in disputed territory, Obama walked out of his meeting with Netanyahu at the White House for a private dinner. He asked Netanyahu to call him if anything new could be talked about. This was viewed as deeply embarrassing to the Prime Minister. Concerned that their conversations would be eavesdropped on the phone lines, the Prime Minister and his advisors left the White House for the Israeli Embassy where they could talk in private.

The expectations of the Obama administration was clear, they expected a freeze on all building projects in Eastern Jerusalem. The official response of Israel was they could build anywhere in Jerusalem that they desired to build.

\

## CORRESPONDING CATASTROPHIES

After carefully monitoring American /Israeli interests over the years, it was in the *spring of 2011* that I took note of Jerusalem entering the negotiation process. I was immediately concerned for our nation's safety! *"As long as the Lord is for us, who then can be against us,"* was Paul's counsel to the Roman Christians. I was anxiously waiting to see what may happen to us if God was not pleased with our actions concerning Jerusalem.

**FEMA's** (Federal Emergency Management Agency) website has listed **86 major disaster declarations** for the United States in 2011 as of September and I hope to highlight several of the remarkable tragedies our nation has incurred thus far on the way toward *peace*. Keep in mind, we must be a true friend to Israel and support her. We should not be responsible to weaken her through forced land attritions.[1]

---

## THIS IS PERSONAL

As I mentioned earlier, I could not understand why the leaders of this country did not personally bear the brunt of disobeying God's promises concerning Israel until I realized that we are a *representative government* and whatever our leaders do in office, we are ultimately responsible because we chose them to represent us.

## TUSCALOOSA, ALABAMA

The most extreme and violent tornado outbreak *EVER RECORDED* and popularly referred to as **"2011 SUPER OUTBREAK"** occurred from April 25-28, 2011. In a three day period, **336 TORNADOES** were confirmed in 21 states with Alabama receiving the worst damage of all. One giant tornado one mile wide cut through Tuscaloosa, Alabama. The city was devastated but fortunately the *University of Alabama* was spared any structural or major damage.[2]

---

## JOPLIN, MISSOURI

Another notable storm to touch our land in the spring of 2011 was the tornado that took aim at downtown Joplin, even going down Main Street itself! The May tornado was the deadliest tornado to hit the country since 1957. It required well over 2 billion dollars to rebuild this one city alone. Though unconfirmed, the St. John Medical Center was moved four inches off its foundation and many died there.[3]

## MAJOR WILDFIRES:

The year 2011 is the year Jerusalem began to come into focus in the U.S. resolve to end the Middle East conflict. *And this happens to be the year that more disasters have visited our nation than is ever recorded or* **remembered.**

No rain in Houston, Texas since January of 2011 as of September 1 and wild fires have been burning all over that state even forcing Rick Perry, a contender for the Presidency to leave the campaign trail and deal with the fires. At the time of this writing, over 1500 homes have burned in Texas. *The unprecedented storms that have hit major metropolitan areas cannot and should not be ignored as coincidence!* We have taken it upon ourselves to place Jerusalem up for grabs as a background for negotiations to begin anew in the Middle East.

## 2011 EASTCOAST EARTHQUAKE: VIRGINIA/WASHINGTON DC-AUGUST 23

A 5.9 magnitude earthquake hit the nation's capital on August 23rd and caused cracks in the *Washington Monument*. The phrase, "PRAISE BE TO GOD," is inscribed on top of the tall structure and was meant to receive the morning's first rays of sun. The *National Parks Service* spokesman reported cracks near the top of the tallest stone structure in the world and has closed to the public indefinitely.[4]

In a revised report and after sending for professional rock climbers from Alaska to survey the monument, damage is much worse than previously thought with 1 ¼ inch cracks near the top of the structure. As a result of *Hurricane Irene* just days later, a large amount of water poured into the structure. At the time of this writing, the interior elevator only runs approximately half-way to the top.

## CRACKS DISCOVERED IN 3 NEW D.C. AREA BRIDGES

In an article published in the *Washington Post* on October 18, 2011, it states that inspectors have found hairline cracks in 3 newly-built overpasses on the Intercounty Connector. This will require parts of the concrete piers be reinforced immediately and perhaps rebuilt. Inspectors for the Maryland State Highway Administration discovered the cracks last week. The 2.56 billion dollar highway's 7.2 mile western segment opened in the spring of 2011 and carried a shelf-life of approximately 6 months![5]

The bridges are still functioning at this point. Additionally, the quake damaged 3 of 4 corner spires on the central tower of the *Washington National Cathedral* along with damage reported at the *Smithsonian*.[5]

## HURRICANE IRENE:

Just days after the August 23rd East Coast earthquake, a slow moving storm hit the *Outer Banks of North Carolina* producing the most devastating water event in over a century. Extensive flooding was reported in Vermont, New York, and New Jersey.

This storm affected more people than any storm in memory. The first landfall was reported near the Outer Banks of North Carolina wiping out property and isolating *Cape Hatteras* from the Outer Banks. The access bridge was totally destroyed and a ferry system put in place.

Irene made her second landfall near *Little Egg Inlet in New Jersey* on the morning of August 28 becoming the **first hurricane to make landfall in the state since 1903!**

*Eastern Upstate New York* and *Vermont* suffered the worst flooding in centuries. States of Emergency were declared for much of the East Coast including *North Carolina, Virginia, Maryland, Delaware, District of Columbia, Pennsylvania, New Jersey, New York, Connecticut, Rhode Island,*

*Massachusetts, Vermont, New Hampshire, and Maine.* There is no way to write about the devastation, loss of life, and property this storm caused right on the heels of the earthquake that shook the entire East Coast only days before![6]

## UNITED NATIONS GETS TOUGH ON ISRAEL- March 30, 2011

## U.N. SUFFERS INNUMERABLE AND UNEXPLAINABLE TRADGEDIES ALL IN THE VERY SAME WEEK

This book is intended to showcase America's dealings with Israel and the resulting divine warnings. The United Nations however is an international organization that is mostly funded and therefore heavily influenced by the *United States.* I have been following closely the unusual calamities that have encompassed the United Nations following a demand on behalf of *"Many nations,"* by Secretary-General Ban Ki-Moon. The request was for Israel to surrender designated properties including East Jerusalem for the purpose of establishing two capital cities one for Israel and one for the Palestinians.

## TIMELINE: March 30, 2011–U.N. SECRETARY-GENERAL'S SPEECH

Here are excerpts of speech the Secretary-General gave during a regional meeting in Uruguay. He said, *"The target date for completing the Palestinian's two-year State-building program is fast approaching. The occupation that started in 1967 is morally and politically unsustainable and must end...The Palestinian's have a legitimate right to the establishment of an independent and viable State of their own... A way must be found for Jerusalem to emerge as the capital of two states, Israel and Palestine with arrangements for holy sites acceptable for all."* [7]

**March 31, 2011: ON THE NEXT DAY: Radiation fears sink seafood sales in Ban Ki-Moon's native South Korea.** This was a result of the Japanese Fukushima Daiichi nuclear complex that was damaged on the March 11, 2011 *tsunami*. Workers were using a milky bathwater dye to determine the path that the radioactive water would take.[8]

**March 30-31, 2011**: *The United Nation* mission in Congo is charged with protecting civilians in a conflict-torn country where 1,000 were found dead.

**April 1, 2011: On the SECOND DAY after speech;**

It is reported, "The U.N. death toll in an attack on the U.N. compound in northern Afghan city of Mazar-i-Sharif could be as high as 21," United Nations officials told Reuters on Friday." Two were also beheaded and parts of the compound also burned. This is the highest loss of life ever for the United Nations in Afghanistan. (The violence was blamed on an American pastor who burned a Koran, but why would the president of Afghanistan incite his country by making a public statement about the Koran burning?)[9]

**April 4, 2011**: A United Nations official says at least 10 U.N. staff members have been killed in a plane crash in the Congo. "The death toll can rise," says the United Nations spokesman. (An update puts the dead at 32 with most of the deceased U.N peacekeepers and staff.)[10]

**April 6, 2011:** Another public relations blunder for the United Nations when it was reported on this day that a United Nation official backed a *Qaddafi Prize* for Human Rights. The prize was named in honor of Muammar Qaddafi whose efforts to mow down his own citizens prompted an internationally backed no-fly zone. Controversial figures such *as Fidel Castro, Hugo Chavez, and Louis Farrakhan* were also awarded such esteemed prizes.[11]

## BIRTHERS ALL WASHED UP

There is a fringe element in America that keeps alive the notion that our President, who claims to have been born in *Hawaii,* is actually a foreigner born in Kenya, Africa. This of course would nullify his presidency if proven correct. As I have discussed previously, we are a *representative government* and therefore responsible for the way the electorate runs our business.

However, each of our presidents most heavily involved in the Israeli debacle have seen tragedy affect the localities from which they were elected. Additionally, personal loss has also been documented with Bill Clinton suffering Congressional impeachment and George W. Bush leaving office in disgrace. We noted the storm that struck Kennebunkport, Maine, heavily damaged G.H. Bush's vacation home as well.

Additionally, Houston, Texas received untold number of misplaced New Orleans' refugees when they were ordered to be bussed directly from the flooded streets around the Super Dome. Many remained permanently though they were originally expected to return back to Louisiana. Hurricane Rita then struck Texas *3 weeks* after Katrina **causing four years of recovery and federal aid**. The oil fields off Texas and Louisiana were greatly impacted as well and gas prices have never recovered to pre-Rita prices.

Since the spring of 2011, I have often wondered how Hawaii could be untouched by calamities since our current president is always candid about his childhood there. I have documented his reliance on failed policies in regards to Israel.

My family enjoyed the *Hawaiian Islands* recently when my youngest son was invited to play in the *Hawaii Collegiate Baseball League*. During that visit I met people at the ball games that were proud of the fact that our current president had attended a renowned private school on the *Big Island* where he grew up.

Horrific news began to be reported on October 24, 2011 that Hawaii was in the direct path of a **sea of garbage** afloat since the **Japanese Fukushima Tsunami struck in the spring of 2011**. A Russian tanker-pilot was willing to update scientists that have been tracking the trash as to its present location.

The massive amounts of material that washed into the Pacific from Japan's coast and heading for America is reported to be *twice the size of Texas*! Up to 20 million tons of garbage heading for Hawaii and California's West Coast much faster than anyone predicted.[12]

**This is an environmental disaster that is in slow motion and began to take aim at the United States within the time frame of**

the Obama offensive to pressure Israel to give up East Jerusalem!


~Headlines on January 18, 2013

"Fukushima Debris Hits Hawaii."  Reuters Times reports that debris set adrift by the 2011 Japanese tsunami has made its way to Hawaii, "Triggering concerns over the unknown effects of the radiation it may carry from the meltdown of the Fukushima reactor." LiveScience, according to the same article says, "Although an estimated 70 percent of the tsunami debris sank offshore, millions of tons of wreckage are still adrift and slowly making landfall."

# 'BY PERSEVERENCE, THE SNAIL MADE IT INTO NOAH'S ARK.'

C.H. SPURGEON

# CHAPTER V

# *X-FACTOR*

There is a popular television program that began in England and found its way to the United States known as *"The X-Factor."* This show seeks out talent from ordinary people who are as yet undiscovered. Their stated purpose is to find someone who has star quality. Jerusalem is a city with star quality! It was a star that personally led three Middle Eastern kings to this desert land in search of the *"Anointed One"* and landed them in Bethlehem over 2000 years ago.

**"Covered in Oil."** **Oil** in the Bible is always symbolic of **Anointing Oil.** The Anointed ones were separate from the common and always considered holy unto

The Lord. ***Jerusalem is a city covered in oil!***
Gethsemane, the hill overlooking Jerusalem is full of Olive Trees. "Oil Press," is the meaning and anointing oil is a natural by-product of this tree! Last year, (2012) according to David Lev, writer for Arutz Sheva, Israel produced 18,000 tons of olive oil! It is the only city on earth that God has revealed His eternal intentions. He declared that in the last days He would be known *not* as the God that delivered the Children of Israel from Egypt but the One who restored them to their homeland after scattering them over the face of the earth due to their rebellion.

Anointed city that she is, it is a marvel and wonder that we as a nation would place ourselves squarely at odds with God when it comes to this land. Jerusalem with her adornment of Anointing Oil is separated for a purpose. Further, she is appointed for the destiny of all mankind and separated from all others! We and the nations of the earth should be affixed upon this city because we all have a personal and national destiny related to her! The key will be to remain on the right side of her and of course believe in the Messiah she has produced!

Referring to the End of Time, Yeshua explains that all nations will be gathered before him for final reckoning. All the angels will be with him and he shall sit upon the throne of his glory. **Of course that throne will be situated in Jerusalem!** As a shepherd divides his sheep, he will divide the nations separately. He shall set the sheep on his right hand, but the goats on the left. Note that word, "but," which has awful consequences (Matthew 25:31-46). (emphasis mine)

Then shall the King say to the sheep on his right, "Come you blessed of my Father, inherit the kingdom prepared for you from the foundation of the world." But to the goat nations, he will say, "Depart from me, you cursed, into everlasting fire, prepared for the devil and his angels…".

It is clear that nations will answer for the deeds done against the eternal King of Israel. It is also wise to pause to give thanks to The Lord for allowing our due judgments to occur in this life. Paul the Apostle states that some men's sins are dealt with in this life, and some men's sins follow them to the next.

Once we realize that God has a pro-active interest in Israel, then we can develop a deeper love and interest in them as well. His Divine care for her in spite of her waywardness should inspire each of us to seek the affection of such an amazing Lover-

95

God! Remember the words lamented over her by Jesus of Nazareth, " Jerusalem, Jerusalem, thou that killest the prophets, and stonest them which are sent unto thee, how often would I have gathered thy children together, even as a hen gathers her chickens under her wings, and you would not!" How often, beloved does God woo you to himself and still does to this day. Maybe this book has affected your faith in such a way that causes you to consider where you stand with God at this moment. Know that with all the certitude this book was written, there is an equal passion in God's heart for you that you are just as vitally important and affectioned by the Creator as Israel. Remember, to Abraham, God said, " Through your seed (Christ) shall ALL the nations of the earth be blessed." The choice is yours! The evidence is overwhelming that God loves the sinner and the disobedient even as much as he loves Israel and has provided a remedy that is as old as the Garden of Eden and as universally accepted into, known as the BLOOD COVENANT. This covenant is not entered into by cutting oneself or by sacrificial animals as a substitute for your redemption but with the Precious Blood of God's only begotten Son. One Most Important Biblical Truth is That Without The Shedding of Blood,

There Can Be No Remission of Sin. One call to God on behalf of Jesus' Calvary Transaction will procure a relationship with God known only by Israel since her existence thousands of years ago!

## WAITING FOR MESSIAH

Eastern Jerusalem is an extremely prominent location when it comes to the Judeo-Christian beliefs. It is the very entrance that believing Jews expect their Messiah to return to Israel! He will then enter the Temple located just beyond the wall.

Ironically, Jesus of Nazareth at the height of his popularity, passed through the *"Messianic Gate"* at the eastern wall on his way to the Temple. Multitudes of Jewish people who were in town from all over the world to attend the Feast of Passover were shouting *"Hosanna to the Son of David! Blessed is he who comes in the Name of the Lord!"* In addition to the praises, they were casting their outer garments before him creating a colorful pathway to the Temple! What a sight as palm fronds were being waved at the sight of such a humble man riding on a donkey as Solomon had done some 1000 years before. Kings intent on war and dominance rode into town on stallions but this was the preferred entry for kings that came in humility and peace.

*"Rejoice greatly, O daughter of Zion; shout, O daughter of Jerusalem; behold, the King cometh unto thee; he is just and having salvation; lowly, and riding upon an ass, and upon a colt, the foal of an ass" (Zechariah 9 vs. 9).*

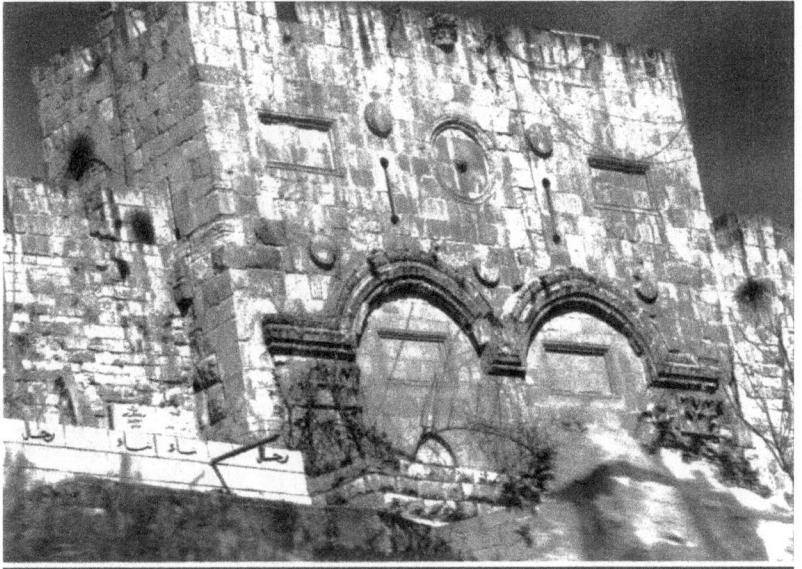

Eastern Gate

This part of Jerusalem was captured from Jordan, Israel's neighbor to the east in 1967 in the *"6-Day War."* Jordan had joined with several other Arab-states in attacking Israel. Jordan was planning to build a resort hotel at the *Eastern Gate.* They had gathered all necessary building materials and construction equipment and were ready to start on site. The day before they were to begin this ambitious project, the war began and all bets were off! The huge *"Eastern Gate"* remains sealed shut today by the government of Israel in anticipation of the Messiah's entry into Mount Zion!

## X-FACTOR

The Greek letter *"X,"* stands **for "*The Anointed One,*"** or **"Christ."** Many well-meaning Christians have been upset over the years during the Christmas season when shop owners would place the holiday greeting, "Merry X-mas", in their store windows. Though it may be true that some indeed intended to insult Christians, it should be understood that whatever their reasoning, the meaning remains the same, **"Merry X-mas" or *"Merry Christmas!"*** [1]

## WHAT MAKES JERUSALEM SO UNIQUE IS THE *"X-FACTOR!"*

It had been chosen before time began to be the central location for God's plan of redemption. Even after Jerusalem had been destroyed by the Babylonian empire in 586 B.C. and Solomon's Temple plundered that God declared the city would one day be rebuilt and the people regathered to their homeland.

*"Behold the days are coming, says the Lord, (again) to the Lord from the tower of Hananel to the Corner Gate...It shall not be plucked up or overthrown any more to the end of the age" (Jeremiah 31:38; 40 amplified).*

## GOLGOTHA

One cannot write about Jerusalem's eternal relevance without referencing a hill many refer to as *"Calvary."* The Latin word, *calvaria* means, *"Place of the skull."* It originated from the Hebrew word for skull, *"gulggulet."* The *Aramaic* version is the one used in the gospel narratives, *"Gol Goatha,"* or **Golgotha**.[2]

Today the location's landscape still resembles the shape of a skull and is regarded as the place where Jesus was crucified. It would have been on one of the main roadways into and out of the city. It was also elevated and all traveling in and out of the city would be able to easily read the inscription Pontius Pilate ordered to be written above Jesus' cross:

*'This is Jesus of Nazareth*
*King of the Jews'*

The Jewish leaders wanted Pilate to write on the inscription that he only claimed to be the *King of the Jews* but Pilate being warned by his wife in a dream that he should not meddle with, *"This good man,"* declared, *"What I have written is what I have written."*

Jewish law required that all executions take place outside the city walls. Interestingly enough, Herod Agrippa later officially included this sacred hill back within the walls (City limits) of Jerusalem.

It should be no small wonder that Christ was sacrificed on *Passover* unofficially within the *confines* of Jerusalem and on the *same* day as the lambs and bulls that would be offered to atone for the sins of the people! Only days before, while Jesus was being interrogated, the priests were busy selecting the perfect unblemished male lambs from the flock for the nations atoning sacrifice.

The spiritual significance of this land can never be understated. The landscape defines it's unique history. It may be said that each one of us has a destiny with Jerusalem. Little wonder that such passions are involved in planning for its future.

Golgotha

# 'WISDOM IS THE PRINCIPLE THING; THEREFORE, GET WISDOM; AND WITH ALL THY GETTING, GET UNDERSTANDING.'

King Solomon -Proverbs 4:7

# CHAPTER VI

# VOTERS GUIDE TO PROSPERITY

"National security and prosperity are inseparably connected with loyalty and obedience to God."[1]

It may seem somewhat preposterous to suggest that if we were to elect true pro-Israel politicians into office that we could somehow as a nation begin to prosper again. **This is exactly what I am saying!** This is not to suggest that we should be divided between two nations, but godly leaders will understand the unique role that Israel has been given on the world stage. Please take notice of what I said, WE CAN *BEGIN* TO PROSPER AGAIN.

Of course, there are serious issues facing our nation that must be addressed but the ancient foundations must be revisited. I am referring to the faith of our forefathers. They came to America from Europe in search of a land where they could freely worship. They could not have known at the time that America, the nation they founded, would play

---

[1]

an integral part in helping to establish the Jews back to their original homeland. **I am hopeful that we are living in the best of days! Not the easiest days, but nevertheless the best.**

I do not believe God has turned His back on America, but it seems we have pulled away our shoulder from Him. Here is one example. The other day someone told me they had visited *Washington D.C.*. They could not help noticing the *Ten Commandments* engraved in the lobby of the *Capital Building*. They noted also some time later while enjoying a movie with friends, the same lobby was filmed but the *Commandments* were cropped out of the film.

This may seem like a small thing, except there has been an orchestrated effort to remove the *Ten Commandments* from courthouses, schools, and wherever they are found. The only problem with our capitalistic and free market society is that we have chosen to leave God out of our national consciousness. Nothing can replace the absolute justice found in the pages of God's Word. Without this compass, anything goes. Everyone has an opinion and an excuse.

## WAKE-UP CALL

Disasters can sometimes be seen as a warning. I am not saying that every time something goes wrong, God is somehow angry with us. I do not believe this for one second. We may never know the reason why many personal tragedies affect us or our loved ones. No one knows with certainty for instance, why one soldier makes it back from war while another doesn't.

We must abstain from the active division of Jerusalem. We have been forewarned in scripture not to tamper with ancient land boundaries. God is gracious to give unmistakable warnings to all who are paying attention.

Let's keep our eyes open and take note of consequences that follow the actions of our national leaders and remember, a *representative government* such as ours requires citizens be responsible for the actions of their elected officials. This will cause us to hold them and ourselves accountable for deviant and offensive actions.

Keep yourself apprised of current events especially those that concern Israel. One of my favorite sources is *"Zion's Hope,"* a free online news publication that is invaluable in getting daily reports concerning the *State of Israel.* So much is not reported in our media and we do well to search things out ourselves. I have found *Jerusalem Post* to be another excellent online daily news source.

## UNDERSTANDING THE TIMES

*"And of the sons of Issachar were men that had understanding of the times who knew what Israel ought to do" (I Chronicles 12:32).*

The sons of Issachar, were the fewest in number of the 12 tribes of Israel, yet they had an understanding as to what they should do. We all know that we are living in dangerous times. More than ever, we need understanding like the sons of Issachar. Things that we have been able to depend on in the past are no longer reliable. Investment strategies have been turned upside down and those who depended on home values to increase are struggling to stay afloat. Families are closer now and more and more will return to their houses of worship in their quest to prioritize their lives.

## A TIME TO SOW

There are many ways to *invest* today. Most important and top of the list; ***invest with your prayers***! As you pray for Israel and one another, true values will be restored and you will once again be sensitized to the feelings of a Loving God.

Another great way to support and bless Israel is to **plan a vacation** there. That way you can experience what God considers to be the best location on earth! There will always be dangers associated with this, but I firmly believe the advantages far outweigh the disadvantages. I am already planning my next visit!

There is no certainty as to the financial stability of nations or kingdoms in the earth today, but one thing I am sure of is that Israel will be here and getting stronger while other nations will fail. While many today are investing in gold and precious metals out of *fear*, the strategy that I am suggesting is based on *faith!*

In the 31st chapter of the book of Jeremiah, and in describing the *New Covenant* with

Israel, one of the terms of the covenant is plainly written.

## START-UP NATION

*"Behold, the days come, says the Lord the city (Jerusalem) shall be built to the Lord..."*
*"{It} will not be plucked up or thrown down any more forever"(Jeremiah 31:38, 40).*

**In uncertain times we need to look for those things that are solid, and growing, and enduring.** This passage states that Jerusalem will undergo a building program that will be sustained forever.

One of the benefits of God's Word is that we know what is coming ahead of time! We know that if God promised us a Savior that would one day be born in Bethlehem-Judah and then He fulfills that promise, we have no recourse but to hold onto His future promises. Jesus promised His return on a day that we **least expect**. *Today* probably fits that description for most of my readers!

The opportunities for us and our children to live peaceably and prosperously depend largely on how we view our future and how we select leaders. *It is* possible to have hope and a bright future. Perspective, like the sons of Issachar demonstrated is the need of the hour!

At this particular juncture, they advised their neighbors to make David their king. They had the ability to advise the nation in matters relating to the sowing and reaping of crops as well as in understanding public affairs. They carefully observed timing and were therefore qualified to make decisions based on facts that others were likely to understand.

This book is not about finances or financial prosperity. But gaining an understanding of our times can help us better plan for the future. The Temple in Jerusalem will one day be rebuilt and the daily sacrifices restored. Much silver and gold will be needed for that project, and so I mentioned to a friend of mine back in 2002 that this investment will one day go through the roof. He listened and bought 40,000 dollars worth of gold coins and in today's market should be worth nearly a quarter of a million dollars! He now operates his own company.

## PAUL'S COUNSEL FOR END-TIMES

" *Charge them that are rich in this world that they be not high-minded nor trust in uncertain riches but in the Living God, who giveth us richly all things to enjoy; That they do good, that they be rich in good works, ready to distribute, willing to communicate; Laying up for themselves a good foundation against the time to come, that they may lay hold of eternal life" (1Timothy 6: 17-19).*

God has blessed our nation as long as we put our trust in Him. We can remain prosperous as a nation as long as we honor God with our allegiance to His promises. We may not like some of the things Israel does as a nation and may not approve of certain ways or things they do, but when it comes to their security and their promised inheritance, let us always come down strong and with conviction on Israel's side! We can no longer assume that if a candidate says that he or she is a Christian or a Jew that they automatically will get these matters correctly.

*NOTE: AT THE TIME OF THIS WRITING, AND AT THE HEIGHT OF THE 2011 HURRICANE SEASON, THREE HURRICANES, KATIA, MARIA, AND NATE APPEARED around September 9th. All three were expected to make their way to the U.S. coastlines.)*

*Notice was taken by the author that the U.S. President showed strong solidarity with Israel following attacks on the Israeli Embassy in Cairo, Egypt. All three storms changed projected paths and missed our homeland. Katia especially would have been devastating with a projected storm track thought to make landfall at the weakened Outer banks of North Carolina and proceed up the recently flooded Northeast.*

*It should be noted that for over a year, there were no major catastrophes or record breaking events and neither were there any meaningful negotiations with Israel from the current administration. Further, the "Road Map to Peace," has never been mentioned again in national or international dialogue.*

## HURRICANE SANDY- *October 22, 2012*

*Just when I thought my work was done here and enough occurrences documented to help my readers determine for themselves as to a Divine purpose in these matters, a storm referred to as a SUPER STORM, surges onto the Democratic stronghold of New Jersey! But what possibly could be taking place in the backdoors of governmental Middle-East policy that this might be tied to? It didn't take long following this monstrosity for friends and colleagues to inform me of the Israeli/United States connection to yet another record breaking event!*

***On the same day*** *former President Jimmy Carter was in Israel meeting with Palestinians and lambasting Israel for their plight, SANDY was forming the first leg of a three-fold monster storm that attacked the shores of New York and New Jersey. Carter also made good on a promised threat to bring up a United Nations resolution in November recognizing Palestine with Jerusalem as its capital to be shared with Israel. No one will ever know the impact this storm had on the presidential elections that would take place in just one month.*

## LIBYA *9/11/2012*

*On September 10, President Obama was reported to have snubbed Prime Minister Netanyahu's request for a meeting at the United Nations to discuss Iran's nuclear ambitions. On the following day, 4 United States Consulates were killed in Benghazi including Ambassador Christopher Stevens in an attack by an Al-Qaeda affiliate. This*

114

*turned out to be a public relations disaster for the administration who initially blamed an anti-Mohammed filmmaker for being unprepared to deal with the terrorist assault. As of one year later, there still have been no arrests in connection with the incident.*

## THE BEAST - *MARCH 19, 2013*

*White House releases a map of Israel the day before President Obama is scheduled to tour Jerusalem. The only problem is what's missing on the map! Jerusalem, Judea, Samaria, and the Golan Heights! These areas are depicted as non-Israeli territory!* **ON THE VERY NEXT DAY, MARCH 20,** *You can't make this stuff up, The Beast, the vehicle used by our presidents and known for its bells and whistles breaks down! He was in Tel Aviv and would have travelled to Jerusalem which in essence doesn't even exist on the map of his host's country! Apparently regular fuel instead of diesel was added to the tank. A helicopter was deployed and got the job done.*

## BOSTON BOMBINGS – *APRIL 15, 2013*

***On the day*** *Secretary of State John Kerry returns to Washington from his Middle-East peace trip and after pressuring Israel back to the table, two bombs explode on the Boston Marathon route! Even though one would be hard-pressed to find information on the partial halt to Israel's building in East Jerusalem and parts of the West Bank, the Washington Times reports on April 12 that Israel has a secret peace plan to QUIETLY halt building plans.*

'I BELIEVE THE ENTIRE BIBLE COVER TO COVER TO BE THE WORD OF GOD; I EVEN BELIEVE THE COVER, '*HOLY BIBLE*'

Andy Elms

# CHAPTER VII

# THE NEW JERUSALEM

Jerusalem will one day undergo a brand new makeover according to scripture. But what should we expect for her in the near term? Following is a brief summary of how things were, how they are today, and what we can expect going forward.

## PAST

Abraham lived his life in search of *this* city and though he lived in tents as a stranger on the land, he died without ever possessing it. His faith in God's promise to grant his children the land for an eternal inheritance still burned in his heart even as he died.

*"By faith he sojourned in the land of promise, as in a foreign country, dwelling in tents with Isaac and Jacob (Israel), the heirs with him of the same promise;* for *he looked for a city which has foundations whose **builder** and **maker** is God." (Hebrews 11:9-10). (emphasis mine.)*

The history of Israel must remain unaltered by those who oppose her existence. Never has a nations past, present, and future been adamantly denied by so many world leaders as it is today. How is it that the truth about Israel conjures up such negative emotion?

It has been shown that Israel desires peace with her neighbors and has returned any land possessed by war that did not rightfully belong to her. Whatever the reason, truth must never be repressed. Truth is like a beach ball pressed beneath the surface of the water, eventually *it will* resurface! Both the glory and agony days of Israel have been recorded for all to see and wonder. Why does she always re-emerge prominently on the world stage after being left for dead? Why does her destiny include each and every one of us and why shouldn't we care? How does she figure in our future as a nation?

## PRESENT

Today may be described as the most dangerous and trying time for this tiny nation. She is as an island surrounded by shark infested waters. This heinous and unfounded hatred is overcome by the *love of a grateful kingdom*! This kingdom, though yet unseen

120

is in the heart of every believer who calls the Jewish *messiah*, Yeshua (Jesus), both Lord and King.

America has been enriched by the enduring relationship with Israel over the decades. There is no indication that this friendship and mutual respect will diminish but on the contrary, in spite of several missteps, the bond is bound to strengthen.

When one considers Israel's determination to survive and her hope for the future, one cannot help but be rewarded with an even greater faith. What God will do for one, He will do for another. Now let's have a look at Israel's future and see how it relates to the destiny of us all.

## COVENANT KEEPER

Covenants which cannot be broken have been made by God with Israel. No matter political correctness or world opinion, some things cannot ever be tampered with.

Jeremiah declared a *new covenant* that God would one day make with them. It will be different from older covenants made when He took them by the hand and led them out of Egypt. They broke that covenant, and a new one was fashioned.

*"Behold the days come, saith the Lord, that I will make a new covenant with the house of Israel...not according to the covenant I made with their fathers...I will put my laws within them, and upon their hearts will I write it."* (Jeremiah 31:31-33).

Jesus came to Jerusalem and offered this *new covenant to the Jews.* He further explained how it worked when he said, that if a man *even looked* upon a woman in order to lust after her, then he had already committed adultery *in his heart.* He was referring to those who have entered into covenant relationship with God through faith in Christ and therefore violate the laws subsequently imprinted upon their heart.

## FUTURE

Jerusalem is described by John in a vision while banished to an island for following *Jesus.* His famous letter was written while there on the isle called "*Patmos.*" The following is his description of *Jerusalem* at the end of the age;

*"And I, John saw the holy city, New Jerusalem, coming down from God out of heaven, prepared as a bride adorned for her*

*husband; And he carried me...and showed me that great city...the city was pure gold like glass...; The foundations of the walls of the city were garnished with all manner of precious stones...and the twelve gates were twelve pearls...and the streets were pure gold." (Revelation 21:2, 10, 18, 19, 21).*

**According to Ezekiel 36, the whole world will sanctify God's great name after they see Him sanctified in the Jewish nation. And then He will cleanse them (The Jew) from all impurities and verse 26 says, "A new heart also will I give you: and I will take away the stony heart out of your flesh, and I will give you a heart of flesh.  And I will put My Spirit within you... and you shall dwell in the land I gave your fathers; and you shall be my people and I will be your God."**

Today, Israel is in the battle for her life. Her *very existence* should serve to prove God's *Word* to be authentic.  If not for God's defense of her, she would've already been decimated beyond recognition.  We will do very well as a nation to remain her most trustworthy supporter!  *If not, God will raise up another to take our place.*

## SOWING AND REAPING

To say that America is in perpetual decline
can be no further from the truth. One only
needs to recall the agricultural law of *sowing
and reaping*. This law applies to almost every
area of life. If we sow to the wind, we shall
reap a whirlwind.  If we sow kindness,
kindness is returned. If generosity, it finds its
way back and so on.  So, the same process
that has pulled us down will be the one that
makes us once again soar with eagles!

Sowing repentance and humility is the
genuine need of the hour. The writer of 2nd
Chronicles 7:14 says,

*"If my people, who are called by my name,
will humble themselves and pray and seek my
face and turn from their wicked ways, then
will I hear from heaven and will forgive their
sin and will heal their land."*

Can anyone honestly say that God has left
off protecting Israel?  He has done so for
thousands of years and has protected the
*United States* for just over two hundred years.

For those who have never felt the need to
answer the call to repent and ask forgiveness,
this could be your moment. It would be easy
to close our ears and heart to such an

124

invitation towards humility. But notice the reward that follows confession; *"I will forgive their sin and will heal their land."* This is exactly the need for our nation at this time. We need a healing for our land! Instead of our land yielding the fruits of prosperity and abundance, the signs on the horizon are for more heartache. The message of this book is that it doesn't have to be this way. We are always on the precipice of forgiveness and healing, the choice is up to us.

## MARANATHA
**~Even so, come, Lord Jesus**

---
---

'I HAVE PUBLISHED WITH THE VOICE OF THANKSGIVING, MAKING KNOWN ALL THY WONDROUS WORKS.'

(Psalms 26:7)

---

# EPILOGUE

The hype of *global warming* and *climate change* surrounding our lives on a daily basis can only be meant to confuse and turn our attention away from things that truly matter. The problems facing our country cannot possibly be only weather related as we have been told. We should always look for the root cause and this book gives a glimpse into a carefully documented cause and effect proposal. I am sure many will not agree with my premise much less my assessment of facts presented but if a level of awareness was raised, then I have accomplished a lot.

This personal story will give understanding as to the focus of my life for the past *37* years, and how the aforementioned events have been my privilege to share with you.

## ENCOUNTERING THE MESSIAH

Early one morning at the age of nineteen and while riding on Pontchartrain's Lakeshore drive in New Orleans, Louisiana, I had my

127

first encounter with Jesus. This occurred in the spring of 1975 and on the day that Christians celebrate Palm Sunday, my girlfriend and I saw a vision that forever would change my life!

As we were gazing at what appeared to be a full moon over the lake and black clouds slowly drifting from left to right over the brightness of the light, an image slowly came into full view. Suddenly we were looking at the face of Jesus in a portrait of clouds and it was perfectly centered in the glow of a full moon. The "*Halo*" I had grown accustomed to appreciating as a young *Catholic* schoolboy was surrounding His countenance and His eyes shone as a flame of fire so bright and penetrating to the core of my soul that I quickly looked away in horror! I could not bear His convicting gaze into my heart. I was certain He knew all of my past sins, and I was horrified. I was able to glance back once or twice and just in time to see the image of Christ in a cloud move completely out of sight. A dark cloud moved in behind it, and never was the image of Jesus visible again.

I knew for the first time in my life that a battle was going on for my soul and everything in me was choosing Jesus and light instead of the evil that I had known. It is important for my reader to be aware that

Satan desires to keep every soul in the grip of unbelief and fear *but Jesus is praying strong and passionate prayers for you!*

## FRATERNITY OF "S I N"

Allow me to digress for a moment. During my high school years, I was invited to join a fraternity consisting of several different schools. The name of this fraternity was "SIN (SIGMA IOTA NU)." Though the letter "S" was spelled with what looks like a backwards "E", it was pronounce as an "S." I realize that fraternities are more college-oriented today and I was only a sophomore in high school at the time but I had a friend whose older brother was a member willing to sponsor me. I shall never forget after successfully pledging and being accepted as a full-fledged member, receiving a golden brown jersey with the letters "*S I N*," written in Greek on the front. I truly thought I had arrived and I can remember it being the most important thing in my life at the time. I remember wearing that shirt every day of my life, and I'm sure my mom remembers this as well!

We would play tackle football without any equipment against rival fraternities and I can not remember too many games we played

129

without an ambulance parked at one end of the field. I personally witnessed our president, Johnny, a huge 300 pound plus guy take his forearm to the back of one of our opponents after a play was ruled over by the officiating crew. You could actually hear the bones in his neck crack. I have no idea what became of that poor guy.

My most regrettable moment during those years was a ritual that our team performed before each game. We would gather into a circle and begin to shout as loud as we could to intimidate the other team. The cheer was a blood curdling blasphemy calling out Jesus Christ as the worst expletive you could ever imagine! I remember looking up to the sky and after shouting with them, "*Sin Once, Sin Twice*," refraining from the blasphemous part ending in "Holy(expletives)... *Christ!*" I honestly could not understand why these young men had such hatred in their hearts for Him. Nevertheless, I was with them, a part of them, and felt completely responsible by associating with them. I wondered what was becoming of my life. Things got far worse after this, and I would be uncomfortable to go into any details.

As a child I was fairly religious. I would ride my bike to the Catholic priest's residence and request a bottle of holy water which was simply a small glass bottle of water that had been blessed by him. I would take this to my room and apply the holy water to my forehead as I entered or left my room. Once I wore a scapula around my neck day and night because I had been told that if you died while wearing it, you would go straight to heaven and not have to make a detour to a holding place called *purgatory*!

I tried out for altar-boy as a young lad but unable to understand the *Latin* Mass, I was flatly rejected. I vented my frustration on one of the boys in my second grade class that did get accepted. Unfortunately for him, I attended a party in his honor only to rough him up a bit. I have to tell you honestly it felt good and it helped me to realize *I wasn't quite ready for altar work.*

Back to my story. Upon experiencing Jesus in a new and living way, the only thing my girlfriend and I knew to do was to do what we always did, go dancing at the lounges and discos every night! The only difference was we wouldn't have any mixed drinks. I found out then that bartenders charge as much for a straight up coke or sprite as they do for whiskey or gin!

Christians soon entered our lives unexpectantly when my friend was asked to stand in their wedding. She was encouraged to attend their church one Sunday but didn't want to attend without me. She attended anyway alone and experienced the purity and joy that I would eventually experience.

Then one evening on our way out to the clubs, by divine chance, she had a craving for a soft-drink. To my surprise, her church friends were having dinner there at the pizzeria and some even came out to invite me to church. I shall never forget the sense of guilt and utter worthlessness I experienced that night as I realized for the first time I was still not right with God. I accepted their kind invitation and made a commitment to trust Jesus Christ with my past, present, and future! From my heart, I committed my sinful past as well as my life's ambitions. "I'll go where you want me to go, Lord and I'll say what you want me to say." I can not put into words how a life can turn from being undone, empty, and cursed, to a life of fullness, hope, and joy!

I not only believed upon Jesus as the "*Anointed One*" sent by God to forgive me of all my sins but I asked Him to come into my heart and help me to tell others about Him!

I went from caring of no one but myself to taking drunkards and homeless off the streets of New Orleans and into a coffee-shop to feed and encourage them. Before leaving the city, I helped establish a church in the

View Carre better known as the *French Quarter*. I have thus far spoken to men for Christ amongst the poorest and weakest to what I consider some of the greatest.

This next verse of scripture has probably helped more people experience Christ themselves than any other:

*"Because if you acknowledge and confess with your lips that Jesus is Lord and in your heart believe (adhere to, trust in and rely on the truth) that God raised Him from the dead, you will be saved. For with the heart a person believes (adheres to, trusts in and relies on Christ) and so is justified (declared righteous, acceptable to God), and with the mouth he confesses – declares openly and speaks out freely his faith – and confirms {his} salvation." (Romans 10: 9-10). Amplified Version*

## MANY ARE UNAWARE OF GOD'S PLAN OF SALVATION:

*"Jesus answered him (Nicodemus, a Jewish leader), 'I assure you, most solemnly I tell you, that unless a person is **born again** (anew, from above), he cannot ever see – know, be acquainted with [and experience] – the*

*kingdom of God...' Jesus answered, 'I assure you, most solemnly I tell you, except a man be born of water and (even) the Spirit, he cannot [ever] enter the kingdom of God...' 'Marvel not – do not be surprised, astonished – You must all be* **born anew** *(from above)." (John 3: 3, 5, 7).*

I have published this book with a sense of Joy and Destiny and with you in mind. At the age of 19, Jesus CHANGED and SAVED my life. I am now 57 and it was the CLEANSING AGENT OF THE BLOOD OF JESUS THAT MADE THE DIFFERENCE FOR ME! Now I have two questions for you:

Number 1: Do you know Jesus as your Personal Savior and Friend? Hope so answers do not count. This is a yes or no.

Number 2: Would you like to actually know The One who made you and Loved you enough to send a Redeemer? If the answer is yes, then it is my honor to lead you in a life-changing prayer:

Ask Jesus TODAY to forgive you of your sins and to come into your life. Find a place to pray today! Use this simple prayer if you like, "Jesus, I believe you are the Savior sent by God the Father to be sacrificed at Golgotha's Hill as a result of my sins.  I believe you died, and you were buried, and rose again on the third day according to scriptures, ascending to heaven to pray for me at the Father's right hand. Please forgive me and come into my heart, giving me new spiritual life.  Thank you for becoming my Lord and Savior! With your help, I will serve you.  I am now a Christian according to John 1:9  Amen.

Now, if you prayed this from your heart, you have received Jesus into your heart and have all your sins forgiven!  Please tell someone about your **new love** and **new life**. It is important to find a good church in your area where you can learn to pray, share, and grow in your experience.  I would also like to send you a pamphlet that will help ground you in your walk with Christ. My email address is: jerusalemxfactor@gmail.com.

R.A. Cuevas

**NOTES:**

Preface:

1.    Spurgeon, C.H. *"Judgment of the Nations,"* July 12, 1885. NHB Christian Talk Ministries. http//nhbchristiantalk.webs.com/wrathofgodornature.ht m.

2    Jewish Encyclopedia.com; http://www.jewishencyclopedia.com/index.jsp

3.    Jones, Vendyl in an interview, *"Ashes of the Red Heifer."*
Audio (C317), Southwest Radio Church P.O.Box 1144, Oklahoma City, OK 73101.

4.    Koenig, William, *"Eye to Eye, Facing the Consequences of Dividing Israel."* Published by About Him, Copyright 2004 by William Koenig. Excerpts posted on NHB Christian Talk Ministries; http//nhbchristiantalk.webs.com/wrathofgodornature.htm.

Introduction:

1.    Koenig, William, *"Eye to Eye, Facing the Consequences of Dividing Israel."* Copyright 2004 by William Koenig. Published by About Him. Excerpts posted on NHB Christian Talk Ministries; http//nhbchristiantalk.webs.com/wrathofgodornature.htm.

2.    Ibid.
3.    Ibid.
4.    Ibid.
5.    Ibid

Chapter 1

1. Howard, Kevin, *"The Location of the Temple,"* in *Zions Fire,* Volume 22 No.1. (page 25).

2. Ibid. 25
3. Ibid. 27
4. Kenyon, E.W. *"The Bible in the Light of our Redemption."*
5. Hagee, John, "Jerusalem Countdown." Frontline; A Strang Company 2006, 2007. www.frontlineissues.com. (page 84)


Chapter 2

1. Strong, James. *"The New Strong's Exhaustive Concordance of the Bible."* Nashville, Tenn,; Thomas Nelson, 1984.

2. Spurgeon, Charles. *"Judgment of the Nations."* 1885.
3. Wikipedia. En.wikipedia.org/wike/Yitzhak_Rabin.
4. Wikipedia. Enwikipedia.org/wiki/Ariel_Sharon.
5. Washington Post article. " Washington Monument Inspected." October 18, 2011.
6. Jones, Ryan. Article, " Obama to Israel: Apologize to Turkey or Else." Quoted from Yediot Abronot. August 17, 2011. www.freerepublic.com/focus/news/2764908/posts.
7. FEMA, http:www.fema.gov/news/disaster-totals-annual-fema.


Chapter 3

1.Yesha Leaders Write UN, 'Bible Records Israel as Jewish Land.'- A7 Israel News- Israel National News. http://israelnationalnews.com./news/news.aspx143897.
2. Hagee, John, "Jerusalem Countdown." Frontline: A Strang Company 2006,2007. www.frontlineissues.com (page 60).

3.  NHB Christian Talks Ministries;
http//nhbchristiantalk.webs.com/wrathofgodornature.htm.
4.  Wikipedia
5.  Ibid.
6.  Christian Science Monitor.
www.csmonitor.com/.../2010/...israel-rejects-obama-s-call-for-buildi....
7.  Fox News; www.foxnews.com/.../2010/.../record-number-foreclosures-face-chall....


Chapter 4

1.  FEMA, http:www.fema.gov/news/disaster-totals-annual-fema.
2.  Wikipedia.
En.wikipedia.org/wiki/april_25_28,_2011_torna do_outbreak.
3.  Wikipedia.
En.wikipedia.org/wiki//2011_joplin_tornado_out break.
4.  New York Times article, August 24, 2011.
www.nytimes.com/2011/08/25/us/25monumenth tml.
5.  Washington Post, "Hairline cracks found in Intercounty County Connector Overpasses" 2011//10/18.
6.  Wikipedia.
Enwikipedia.org/wiki/Hurricane_Irene_(2011).
7.  Secretary-General. Office of the Spokesman. March 29, 2011.
www.un.org/apps/sg/sgstats.asp?mid=5173.
8.  "Seafood sales sink in S. Korea Due to Radiation Fears". March31, 2011 article by Steve Herman, Voice of America.
9.  Article in Reuters " Up to 20 U.N. Staff killed in North Afghan city," April 1, 2011.
10.  Article, Update 5- "U. N. plane crashes in Congo killing 32"- Reuters.

11.  Article on Fox News Channel, April 6, 2011.
"Rights groups call on U.N. to oust Swiss
official who allegedly backed Quaddai "Prize."
12.  KITV Honalulu, October 19, 2011. " U.H.
researcher predicts Tsunami debris coming
sooner to Hawaii.
http;//www.citv.com/r/29530797/detail.html.


Chapter 5

1.  Christ-Wikipedia. En.wikipedia.org/wiki/Christ.
2.  Golgotha. Catholic Encyclopedia: Mount Calvary.
www.newadvent.org<Catholic Encyclopedia>.
3.  Ibid.


Chapter 6

1.  the New Scofield Reference Bible. Authorized King
James Version. New York-Oxford University Press, 1967. Copyright
1907; Used by permission; page 291.

**Rev. Cuevas is available for speaking engagements.
Contact him at jerusalemxfactor@gmail.com.**
## Additional copies can be purchased by writing to:

## Honor Publishing
## P.O. Box 1825
## Fletcher, NC  28732

www.ingramcontent.com/pod-product-compliance
Lightning Source LLC
Chambersburg PA
CBHW031210270326
41931CB00006B/502